W9-CFG-540

THE KIDS' CAT BOOK

FREE
KITTENS
INSIDE

GRANNY TWINKLE

THE KIDS' CAT BOOK

written and illustrated by
TOMIE DE PAOLA

T 16035

Holiday House · New York

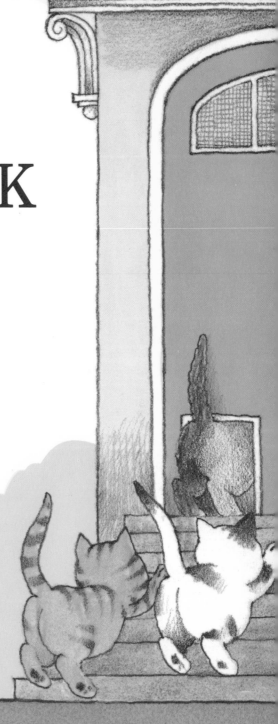

T 16070

For Patrick

Y636.8
1981

Copyright © 1979 by Tomie de Paola
All rights reserved
Printed in the United States of America

Library of Congress Cataloging in Publication Data

De Paola, Thomas Anthony.
  The kids' cat book.

  SUMMARY: Patrick goes to Granny Twinkle's for a free
kitten and learns everything there is to know about
cats—their different breeds, care, place in art and
literature, and history.
  1. Cats—Juvenile literature. [1. Cats] I. Title.
SF445.7.D4   636.8   79-2090
ISBN 0-8234-0365-3

"Right here, I have some nice Siamese kittens. Siamese have dark ears, paws, tails, and faces. These are called points. They have blue eyes and short hair. They like to talk a lot and are great climbers.

"There is a story that Siamese cats were once the royal property of the King of Siam. They were trained to guard the royal palace. Some people say their meows were louder than barking dogs. Others say that the Siamese cats walked the palace walls. If anyone tried to break in, they jumped on their backs."

"Look, those kittens have no tails!"

"They're Manx kittens. They come from the Isle of Man in the Irish Sea. They have arched backs, which gives them a short, round look. In fact, they are round all over—round heads, round faces, and round rumps.

"There are three kinds of Manx tails: RUMPY, which is no tail at all; STUMPY, which is a tail only one to five inches long; and LONGIE, which is a whole tail.

"Manx cats have short front legs and long back legs and sometimes they hop. Once, people thought they were part rabbit."

"Oh, and here are some fluffy Persians. Persians have long, shiny fur, round, round eyes, and big, bushy tails. They were brought to Europe in the late 1500's by travelers from Persia. They were very rare for a long time.

"Persians love to lounge around. They'd rather take a nap than catch mice."

"These kittens have curly hair like poodles'."

"Yes, they are called Rex cats. They are very rare and have a special kind of coat. They look as though they just had a permanent wave at the beauty parlor. Even their whiskers are curly.

"The first Rex cat was discovered in 1950 on a farm in Cornwall, England."

"And here are my favorites—Abyssinians. Abys look like small mountain lions. They are always happy and busy and very quick. Abys have large ears, and even the grown-ups look and act kittenish. They have soft, silky coats and small, bell-like voices. And they are so affectionate!

"Many people call Abyssinians the cats from ancient Egypt."

"Did they have cats way back then?"

"Oh, my goodness, yes! Some experts think the cat was tamed by 3,500 B.C. The ancient Egyptians were the first people to keep cats for pets. They also worshiped cats as gods.

"Because cats could see at night and slept curled up like a crescent moon, the Egyptians believed that the cat saved the world from darkness.

"There is a story about it. Would you like to hear it?"

"Oh, yes. I love stories."

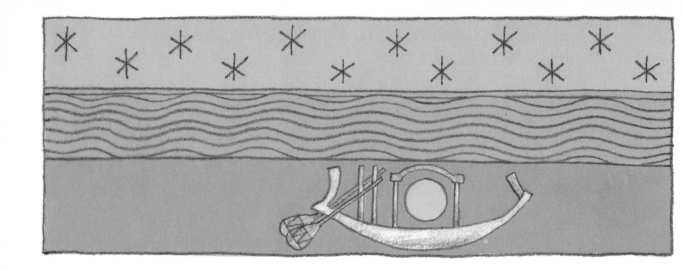

"Every night, when the sun set, it had to travel through the underworld before it could rise again.

"The great serpent of darkness, Apep, lived in the underworld. Each night, the serpent would try to swallow the sun. If it did, the earth would be dark for the rest of time.

"But, luckily for the earth, the great sun god, Ra, would turn himself into a cat and fight Apep. Every night, he would chop the serpent into pieces with his sword.

"And when the sun rose again in the morning, the earth knew that Ra had won his battle once more."

"When I went to the museum, I saw a statue of a lady with a cat's head."

"Ra had a daughter who had a cat's head, and she was called the goddess Bastet. All the Egyptians loved and worshiped her. That's why the Egyptians loved their cats."

"In fact, when their cats died, they buried them all wrapped up in linen strips. They put them in the best mummy cases they could buy. They put tiny mummy-mice and other food in the tombs and cemeteries, too. This was so the cats would have something to eat in the afterworld."

"The Romans found cats in Egypt and, as they conquered the world, they brought cats with them into Europe.

"At first, cats were considered very rare and very helpful. They caught lots of mice and rats. But as cats became more common, they became less valuable. Finally, in the Middle Ages, people thought cats were evil and the helpers of witches. That's why even today at Halloween, you usually see pictures of cats sitting on witches' broomsticks."

"Many cats were killed in the Middle Ages, until the Black Plague came in the 14th century. The plague was brought by black rats from Asia. The people who secretly kept cats were luckier, because the cats killed the rats. So, laws protecting cats were made. Once more, cats began to increase in numbers."

"Then cats became important again, right?"

"Right. In fact, in England during the time of Queen Victoria, many painters and writers put cats in their pictures and stories. There were pictures of cats curled up by fires and in the laps of boys and girls, and even cats looking out of windows.

"Painters wanted to show that cats and happy homes went together."

"Are cats hard to take care of?"

"My goodness, no. Cats are meat-eaters, but they need more than just meat. They need a well-balanced diet, high in protein and fat. They need four times more protein and fat than dogs. So, NEVER feed dog food to cats. It's a good idea to ask your vet what the best diet would be.

"Kittens should be fed two small meals, twice a day. Adult cats should be fed one large meal, once a day. When a mother cat stops feeding her kittens, they no longer need milk. They do need lots of fresh water, though."

"If a cat is an 'inside cat' and doesn't go outdoors, it will need a litter box. Cats are very easy to housebreak. Put the kitten in the box and scratch its paws in the litter. Do this a couple of times. Your kitten will never make a 'mistake' AS LONG AS THE LITTER BOX IS KEPT CLEAN."

LITTER BOX

"When a new kitten—or an old cat—comes to live with you, it should be examined by a vet. The vet will make sure it's healthy and doesn't have fleas, ear mites, or worms. The vet will also give it shots.

"If your cat doesn't eat or play or act like itself for a couple of days, it might be sick. DON'T GIVE IT PEOPLE MEDICINE. Call the vet."

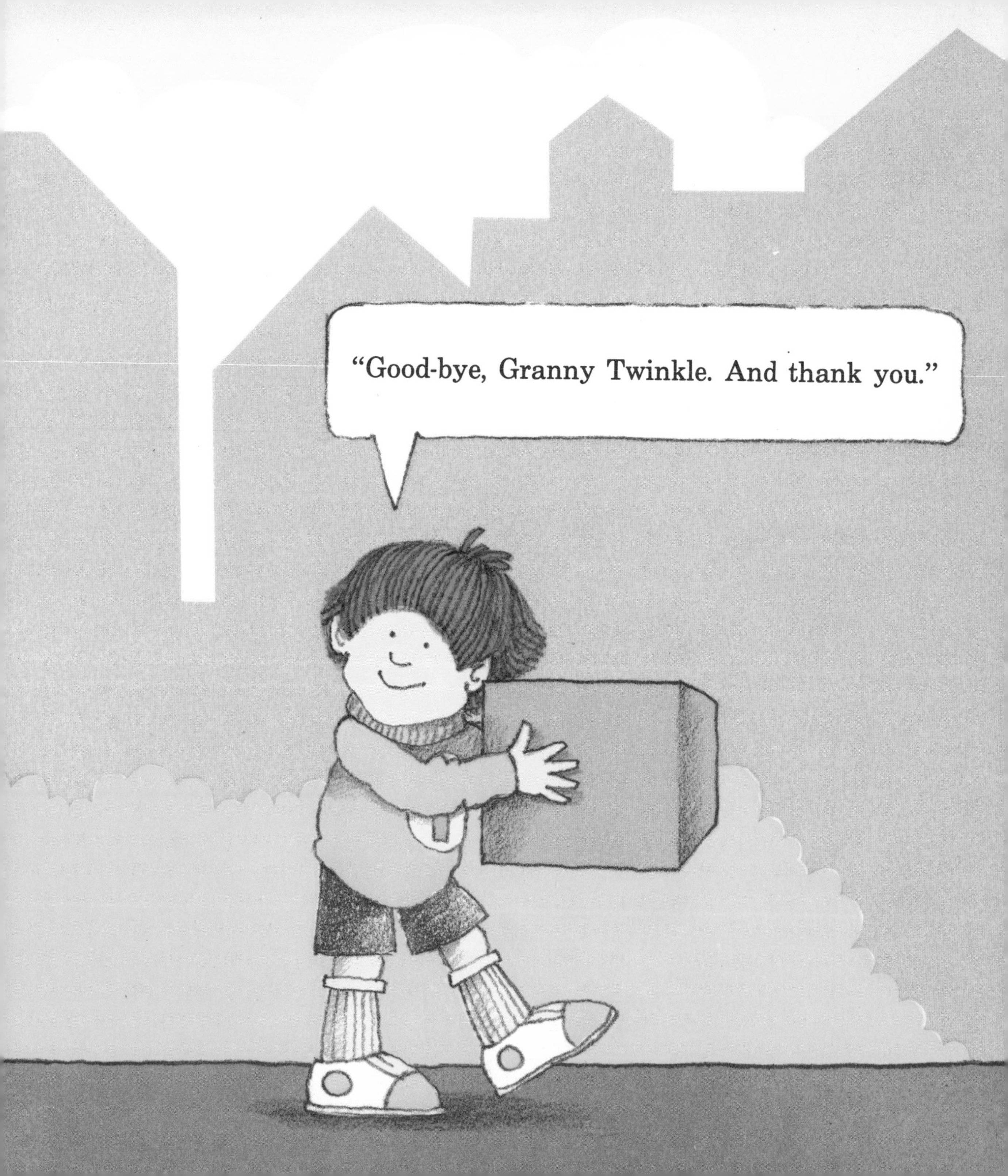
"Good-bye, Granny Twinkle. And thank you."

"Look what I've got!"

FREE KITTENS
EACH
KITTEN GIVEN AWAY
WITH FREE ADVICE
AND
CAT INFORMATION
FROM
PATRICK, THE CAT EXPERT

SOME INTERESTING CAT FACTS

1. All kinds of cats purr, including the big cats—like lions, tigers, and leopards. Purring is caused when the walls of a large blood vessel, *vena cava*, vibrate. This blood vessel runs between the belly and chest.

2. Male cats are called toms. Female cats are called queens.

3. Cats usually land on their feet, even when they fall from great heights. This is one reason people believe cats have nine lives.

4. A tabby cat is a patterned cat that is striped. It can be shades of black, gray, or orange.

5. A tortoiseshell cat is black with patches of orange and cream.

6. A calico cat is white with patches of orange and black. Calicos and tortoiseshells are almost always females.

7. The Egyptian word for cat is *miu*. In China, it is *mao*.

8. 1975 was the Year of the Cat in China. The next one will be in 1987.